CHESTER
THE FUZZY
CHIPMUNK

JENNY SCHREIBER

Jenny Schreiber
Star Valley, WY 83110

In association with
Elite Online Publishing
63 East 11400 South #230
Sandy, UT 84070
EliteOnlinePublishing.com

ISBN: 978-1-956642-66-7 Hardback
ISBN: 978-1-956642-67-4 Paperback

CHESTER
THE FUZZY
CHIPMUNK

JENNY SCHREIBER

Meet Chester the fuzzy chipmunk.

"Chitmunk", comes from the native Odawa (Ottawa) word jidmoonh, meaning "red squirrel".

Chipmunks have also been referred to as striped squirrels, timber tigers, mini-bears, and ground squirrels.

They live in the forest
and in the park.

They are brown with a white stripe.

Chipmunks make various sounds to communicate. There are three recognized chipmunk calls.

The three calls are called the chip, the deeper chuck, and the startle call.

They eat seeds, nuts, fruits, and tree buds.

They also eat grass, fungi, insects, small frogs, worms, and bird eggs.

**Chipmunks can gather
up to 165 acorns
in a day.**

They store and hoard their food for the winter in their burrows.

Eastern chipmunks hibernate in the winter.

Western chipmunks do not hibernate in the winter.

They work and play during the day.

They sleep at night.

They can sleep up to 15 hours.

They are fully grown at 9 months old.

Chipmunks are 18–25 cm (7.1–9.8 in) long, a third of which is the tail.

Chipmunks live in
North America.

Also, in Siberia which is Northern Asia.

They live in coniferous forests, stony areas within forests, and mountains.

THE END

Find More books by Jenny Schreiber

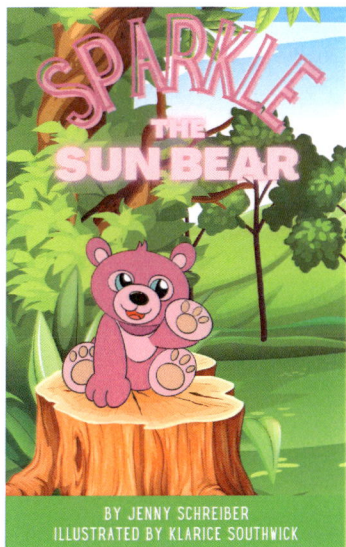

Sparkle the Sun Bear

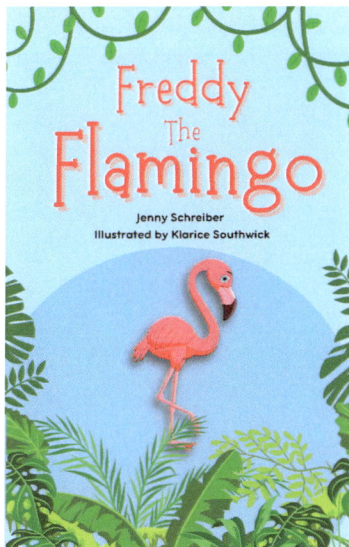

Freddy the Flamingo

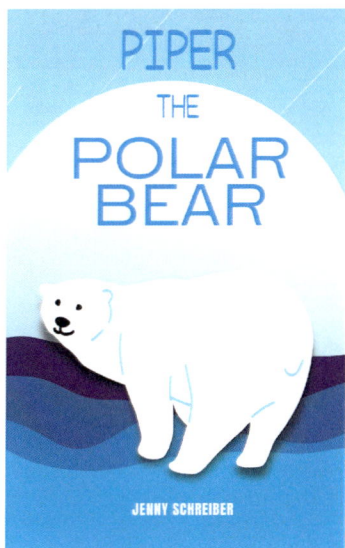

Piper the
Polar Bear

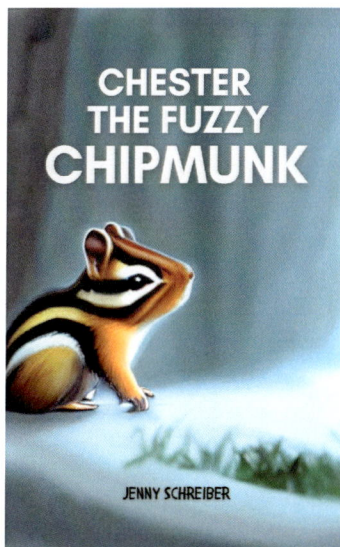

Chester the
Fuzzy Chipmunk

Animal Facts Children's Book Series

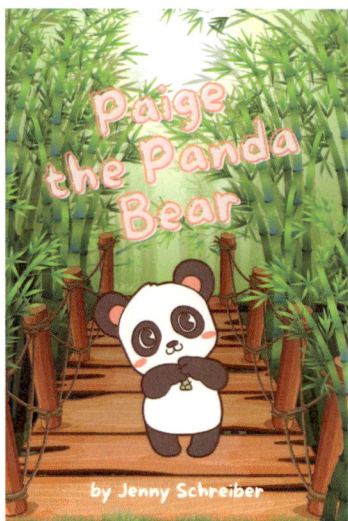

Paige the
Panda Bear

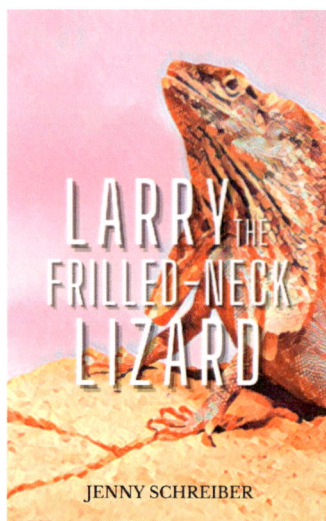

Larry the
Frilled-Neck Lizard

www.ingramcontent.com/pod-product-compliance
Lightning Source LLC
Chambersburg PA
CBRC101142030426
42335CB00007B/202